A devastating step-by step deterioration. . .through ignorance and innocence. . .of all that once was. . .

A realistic day-by-day journey. . .through choices and attitudes. . .of all that can be. . .

Marital Life

Richard R. George

PRESS

Marital Death - Marital Life
by Richard Robert George

Printed in the United States of America

ISBN 9781622308972

Unless otherwise indicated, Bible quotations are taken from the King James Version (KJV). Copyright © 1967 by Oxford University Press.

www.xulonpress.com

DEDICATION

*T*hanks be to God who rescued and restored our marriage many years ago. It is to Him and my wife, Sue, that I dedicate this book for the sake of all who are married.

Once in a while, because of me, but mostly in spite of me, Sue has persevered and somehow loved me anyway.

Table of Contents

CHAPTER ONE

"UNFAIR!"

I grew up in a small town, where everyone knew everybody else's business. It seemed that people were always whispering about my family. They sometimes called my mother names. They said that I was illegitimate. It was even said that my father was a fool.

I was initially rejected by my father. My mother felt disregarded and emotionally scorned for many years after my birth. Because of her fears, she tended to be overprotective of me. I grew up feeling continuously misunderstood. I guess I was always different from my peers. Even my own family questioned my motives and actions. Feeling love and needing love, I tried to please others. My mother *considered me thoughtful. My father thought that I needed to "toughen up." My younger brothers and sisters were jealous and my friends ridiculed me. Life was difficult.*

My father insisted that I learn the family business. He believed in hard work and expected me to someday follow in his footsteps. He died prematurely, and being the oldest, I was expected to care for the family. This was the most emotionally difficult and financially unsettling time for all of us.

While I was good at my trade and worked long hours to provide for the family, I grew up restless, believing that I had much more to offer the world than this.

One day I walked away from it all. I left the family business to the care of my brothers, who I had sufficiently trained. I didn't ask. I didn't explain. I just knew that it was the right thing to do, and the right time to do it. The townspeople thought me irresponsible and inconsiderate of my mother, who had always loyally stuck by me through thick and thin.

The gossip grew worse as I left home entirely. I traveled from town to town and place to place, accused of being an itinerant vagabond by some, and an insane rebel by others.

I was in sales. I communicated ideas, thoughts, principles, and all manner of truths that people desperately needed to hear, understand and apply. I always meant well, but was not always received well. My ideas were fresh, yet aged. While they weren't always entirely new, they were communicated with a somewhat uniquely relevant twist.

I sought to help many, yet it was few who understood. I soon gained a support group of sorts. These were people from varied backgrounds, mostly poor, who somehow believed in me and my ideas. It wasn't because I particularly sought them, as much as they seemed to be seeking me. Funny, I had never experienced this kind of popularity growing up.

But even this temporary popularity had its price. Some people feared me. Some accused me falsely of saying things I had never said. Some sought to hurt me, even physically.

It's strange how the revelation of truth is so penetrating that it is discomforting. And how amazing it is, that if you deliver truth wrapped in love, I mean real, unselfish, totally surrendered, sacrificial love, people are suspect of your motives, spiteful of your success, and hateful of your plans.

Many became so emotionally unnerved by my mere presence that they sought to publicly discredit me. Some became so afraid of my ideas that they plotted to arrest me. And yes, some who I had rescued, helped, and loved dearly, abandoned me when their purposes were not mine.

Finally, in the end, I unfairly paid the ultimate price of integrity. I was shunned, rejected, discredited, laughed at, spit upon, profaned, whipped with nail-laden straps, forsaken, beaten, hammered, and suffocated to death.

My body was dead and buried. But the ideas, hopes, dreams, and assurances that I shared were resurrected, as was I, in such a way that my Spirit and your spirit were blended together when you accepted me and chose to walk in my Truth.

Yes, my child, life is unfair. I will attest to that. But if I had to pay the same excruciating price for your eternal freedom and relationship with me all over again. . .I would do it.

Why? Because you are worth it, and because I love you. . .forever.

You have just read the story of a perfect man, who lived a perfect life. In everything He ever did, He constantly and consistently evidenced overwhelming love, care, and consideration for all He ever met. He prayed for everybody, helped anybody, and healed all who asked, and made them each feel like a "somebody." For all of these immeasurable and incomprehensible efforts, He was rewarded by those who had experienced Him, with hideous and unimaginable inhuman execution.

This is the zenith epitome of "unfair." Frankly, everything else pales in comparison. However, even though none of us can possibly relate to the magnitude of "unfair" that He experienced, we nevertheless do have our own personal life versions.

Some of us have a "father wound" while others have a "mother wound." Most of us have been greatly influenced by our parent(s) or lack thereof. Perhaps "unfair" oozes out of our very souls as life's experiences have saturated us with severe pain and deep disillusionment due to molestation, rape, incest, divorce, death, favoritism, unjust birth order, or just bad timing or bad "luck."

Then we get married. Every couple I've ever married typically has expectations of long term success. I know of no one who utters under his/her breath, "I can't wait for this marriage to die," as they walk down the aisle. That would be absurd. They think that it may be a bit difficult at first (adjusting and all), but it will be a good life together. Prayerfully, a very happy life indeed.

Marriage, the spiritual, legal, emotional, social and psychological union of a man and a woman is the oldest God-ordained institution of mankind. It was instituted by God, before government and before the church. It has been and still is the foundation of unyielding moral bedrock to which any society or culture, (wishing to survive with great success) must pledge its allegiance. History repeatedly records the destruction of all great societies from within; typically beginning with the moral decay of marriage and the family.

Be that as it may, a committed and flourishing relationship between a man and woman in marriage is a fragile thing. Eventually, the pressures and expectations of living with another person presents challenges that seem to never go away. There are the arguments that never get resolved, the decisions without consideration to feelings, autonomous pursuits of fun and relaxation, the "putting first" of other people invading the sanctity of family and intimacy, and endless experiences of hostile body language, as well as aggravated and even nasty tone of voice. Yes, UNFAIR! Men and women were created differently. In the book to follow, while all that is provided in terms of thinking and behavior is accurate, it is sometimes found in the opposite sex. What do I mean by that?

We are many, many, many generations away from the original "gene pool" of Adam and Eve. While men are always "compartmentalized" thinkers, living in "matter moments" (what matters at the moment), women are always "chain-linking" thinkers, living in "multiple matters" (with past, present, and future all mattering at the same time). Men typically "isolate" information while women "integrate" all sorts of data, all at the same time.

While this is always true, there seems to be some deviation, as to what each does first. I think the 80/20% rule should be applied to better understand what's going on.

The 80/20% rule is typically referred to by economists as the "Pareto Principle." It seems that 80% of most business is provided by 20% of the clientele. As an intriguing and pertinent aside, for years churches have claimed that 80% of monies received were provided by 20% of all congregants and 80% of ministry in the church was done by 20% of the people as well. Additionally, in Malcolm MacDowell's book, "The Tipping Point," he mentions that 80% of all beer is consumed by 20% of beer drinkers and 80% of all accidents are by 20% of vehicle drivers. An emergency room doctor recently told me that 80% of all diseases befall 20% of the population.

While all men are compartmentalized thinkers, often lost in a focused world different from a woman's preference, it seems that highly emotional men (usually with a high degree of perfectionism), also have the ability to "chain-link" or integrate dominantly over their ability to compartmentalize (without actually losing that same ability).

While all women are chain-linking thinkers, scanning tirelessly through pertinent (and sometimes not so pertinent) data, it seems that non-emotional women, also have the ability to "compartmentalize" or isolate dominantly over their ability to chain-link (without actually losing that same ability).

The great news is that opposites attract, so they find each other and marry. It is highly significant to understand, so that the reader knows which side of the forthcoming "Marital Death Chart" he or she should be relating to. As the reader goes through the chart, it is possible to have a few role reversals. DON'T PANIC! It is not abnormal! While there are many "staples" of male and female thinking, there has to be some variation. When you consider that genetics, birth order, sex of siblings, single or two parent families, life experiences, and perceptions of reality all play a role, it is amazing that the 80/20% rule still applies.

The "Marital Death Chart" you are about to experience in the next chapter, is a GENERAL description of what the man and woman each think is true. It is designed to create "eye-opening" awareness to get the couple going. Every man and woman in intimate relationship with one another is on this chart somewhere. It is normal to bounce around on it, but dangerous when you keep dropping down and staying down.

Let me share a few stories with you about real people, just like yourself, who have had experience with this chart and how its teaching played out in their lives.

I have changed the names to protect the privacy of the counselees.

Story 1.

Dave and Betty were the 20% exception. He was a highly perfectionistic man who was very creative and had high expectations of his wife, with little affirmation to bestow upon her. He was in total control for many years and often put her down.

Finally, Betty (less emotional and more logical) lost weight, patience, and her fears and began dressing like her teenage daughters. She became unaccountable for large chunks of time, while working in a highly professional environment.

Dave was frantic and called me out of desperation. He was virtually suicidal and became even more smothering of Betty, through spying, accusations, fits of rage, emotional begging, and asking his children to take his side.

They eventually came for counseling (though late in the game), and while she might have eventually responded (as she passed through this critical age and time of her life), his obsessive smotherings and fears of losing her (which he refused to change), became such an obstacle to her wanting to be around him, that she would no longer counsel and eventually divorced him.

Sadly, counseling can only be effective if those people being counseled follow good counsel.

Suffocation, Escape, Encounter, Helplessness, Bitterness, and Hopelessness were overwhelming evidence, as

Dave slid down the slippery slope of "Crying" and "Dying" on the Marital Death Chart you will read shortly.

In like manner, and even faster, Betty exhibited severe Bitterness, Reaction, Fear, Release, Indifference and Hopelessness even more quickly in the Level III "Crying" and Level IV "Dying."

They did not follow the Marital Death Inventory protocol, therefore they didn't stand much of a chance.

Story 2.

Jim and Dana were in trouble and Dana called me for help. While their circumstances were a bit different from most couples, they were clearly failing in the "Trying" Level of the Marital Death Chart, (found in the next chapter) like many other couples typically do.

Jim was pre-occupied and traveling a lot and his priorities were in all the wrong places. Yet he believed he was a good guy and his wife was overreacting to their need for counseling. He was pre-occupied, rationalizing, and breaking down in frustration over his wife's inconsiderations. He was truly in Level II of the chart.

Dana was full of apprehension as she watched him being manipulated by a group of friends, discouraged by their time and distance from each other and feeling emotionally isolated by his apparent obsession with looking at other women. She was in Level II and quickly spiraling toward Level III.

With great persistence she finally persuaded him to come to counseling with her (which is a problem many women encounter with their husbands). After just a few sessions they were well on their way to greater understanding of each other's needs and the reprioritizing of his life, which reenergized her and motivated her to be far more responsive to him. They followed the counseling protocol and their marriage has been wonderfully renewed.

Story 3.

Bill and Bonnie were casual friends of mine. I hadn't actually seen them for awhile, when Bonnie called very upset. It seemed while she believed that they had a good marriage, his thoughts were elsewhere.

Apparently there was a girl in his past that he never got over and often thought about. His esteem had been leveled by recent business reverses and unbelievably he accidentally bumped into this former girlfriend. Somehow all of the wondering, regrets and fantasy became a new reality in his stress-filled existence, as he had another chance with the girl of his dreams.

Because Bonnie and Bill were always candid with each other, he told her the whole story. Bonnie courageously and prayerfully endured the pain that her husband "wanted out" to be with this long-lost love. He was obsessed with her and would continue to see her.

The past with Bonnie was cherished and appreciated, but the future did not include her. He was abandoning the teachings of his faith and the principles of his life.

She called to see if I would try to talk to him to somehow talk some sense into him. She hoped he would meet with me. I was her only hope, because of our friendship.

I immediately called to talk to him about getting together, assuring him that I was not judging him, nor would I condemn him. He grudgingly agreed, reminding me that nothing I could say would change his mind.

We met and talked on several occasions. I lived up to my end of the bargain. There was no judging and no condemning.

Bill had sped from the "Trying" Level through the "Crying" Level and had landed firmly on the last phase of "Hopelessness" of the fourth and final Level, known as "Dying." He was already in emotional divorce and seeking a legal one.

Bonnie, on the other hand, was only on the last phase of "Isolation" in the "Trying" Level. She was hurting and wanted him back.

After some time, much counsel, great opportunity to speak truth into his life, the "scales" began to fall from his eyes and he was no longer blind to Bonnie and how he deeply felt about her.

By following their remedial counseling protocol of knowing how each other should be and what each other should do, through new formation of attitudes and approaches, their marriage was made whole, stronger than before.

As you read the Marital Death Chart in the next section, seek to be honest with yourself and one another. Determine where you are and do something positive about it. Be kind. Be strategic. And remember, just as the three basic principles of success in business are Location. . .Location. . .Location. . .the three basic principles of success in relationships are Communicate. . .Communicate. . .Communicate.

CHAPTER TWO

"MARITAL DEATH!"
(DESTRUCTION BY INNOCENCE)

	"MAN"			"WOMAN"		
	PHASE PROCESS	PRAYER	PERCEPTION	PHASE PROCESS	PRAYER	PERCEPTION
LEVEL I "SIGHING"	NURTURING	"THANK YOU, GOD!"	"SHE'S GREAT!"	NURTURING	"THANK YOU GOD!"	"HE'S WONDERFUL!"
LEVEL II "TRYING"	PRE-OCCUPATION	"GOD BLESS US?"	"HUH?"	APPREHENSION	"GOD BLESS US?"	"WHY IS HE SHUTTING ME OUT?"
	RATIONALIZATION		"IT'S NOT IMPORTANT!"	DISCOURAGEMENT		"HE USED TO BE SO OPEN WITH ME!"
	BREAKDOWN		"WHAT DOES SHE WANT FROM ME, ANYWAY?"	ISOLATION		"HE DOESN'T NEED ME LIKE HE USED TO!"
LEVEL III "CRYING"	SUFFOCATION	"GOD, WHY IS SHE LIKE THIS?"	"SHE WANTS WAY TOO MUCH FROM ME!"	BITTERNESS	"GOD HOW CAN I MAKE HIM SEE?"	"IF HE REALLY CARED HE WOULD BE CONSIDERATE OF ME!"
	ESCAPE		"I'LL NEVER UNDERSTAND HER!"	REACTION		"HE CAN'T TELL ME WHAT TO DO!"
	ENCOUNTER		"SHE'S NOT GOING TO WIN AGAIN!"	FEAR		"HE WON'T CARE! I WON'T CARE!"
LEVEL IV "DYING"	HELPLESSNESS	"LOOK, GOD…"	"NOTHING I DO PLEASES HER!"	RELEASE	"GOD… NEVER MIND!"	"I'VE HAD IT WITH HIM!"
	BITTERNESS		"NO OTHER WOMAN WOULD TREAT ME LIKE THIS!"	INDIFFERENCE		"I WISH HE'D LEAVE!"
	HOPELESSNESS		"I MADE A MISTAKE! I DON'T LOVE THIS WOMAN!"	HOPELESSNESS		"HOW COULD I HAVE BEEN SO WRONG? HE'S TERRIBLE! I COULD NEVER LOVE HIM!"

"THE POISONING"

MARITAL DEATH

"I want a divorce!" "I don't love her!" "I can't stand him!" Sound familiar? MARITAL DEATH is a "destruction by innocence" that sneaks up on unsuspecting couples. This communication poisoning process is not uncommon to any of us. No matter how hard we personally believe we are relationally trying, our perception, which is our reality, is often totally foreign to what our loved one believes.

The MARITAL DEATH Chart is a descending instrument used to measure and determine how counselees can know where they are in their relationship, so that they may be given relational tools. These tools will take the marriage back to satisfactory levels of wholeness.

When couples regressively move down the chart camping in each place for a long time, the marriage is in serious trouble. Let's look at the chart:

LEVEL I (SIGHING)

In the NURTURING phase, both are greatly pleased and seem to understand each other in most everything.

LEVEL II (TRYING)

In PREOCCUPATION this "compartmentalized-thinking" husband receives his esteem from many places and inadvertently stops talking and listening to her. In APPREHENSION, this "chainlink-thinking" wife feels shut out and lonely. She tries to tell him.

In RATIONALIZATION he thinks she's overreacting. In DISCOURAGEMENT she feels frustrated and helpless. She increases the pressure to restore what once was.

In BREAKDOWN he rebels against her negativity. In ISOLATION she feels unneeded and desperately detached.

LEVEL III (CRYING)

In SUFFOCATION he feels unappreciated with his manhood threatened. In BITTERNESS she feels unloved, angry, and emotionally destitute.

In ESCAPE, his damaged ego makes him withdraw to his job, hobbies, or another woman. In REACTION, she rebels against his authority and becomes emotionally unaccountable to him.

In ENCOUNTER, his need for ego mastery dominates to rescue his manhood. In FEAR she senses that they are at the point of no return.

LEVEL IV (DYING)

In HELPLESSNESS he senses her quitting on him and feebly tries, to no avail. In RELEASE, she emotionally "lets him go" and doesn't care.

In BITTERNESS, greatly angered by her unforgiving ways, he sees her undeserving of him. In INDIFFERENCE, she wants him out of her life.

In HOPELESSNESS, he believes he never really loved her. In HOPELESSNESS, she feels deceived, betrayed, and out of love.

MARITAL DEATH INVENTORY

Introduction: Each person in a marriage has his/her own individual perceptions of the relationship. Even though your spouse may see things differently, nevertheless it is what they believe to be true. Men, after you have fully evaluated yourself ask your partner what they think about these "Marital Death" symptoms and alter her perceptions by making minor adjustments in your behavior. While you cannot personally change her, you can change yourself, thereby effecting change in her perceptions. These changed perceptions create a new reality and responsiveness.

MEN. . .ASK YOURSELF. . .

TRYING LEVEL	DO YOU. . .	THEN SEEK TO. . .
	1. Sometimes "zone out," preoccupied with work or other things that interest you? **(PRE-OCCUPATION)**	1. Remember that your wife feels significant and safe when she knows she is first in your life. Try "zoning-in" on her. She needs your focus often. Be romantic, even if you don't have the need. She does.
	2. Sometimes become selective in what you tell her? Do you ignore details of your day, thinking them unimportant? Do you try to protect her from information that will cause her to worry? **(RATIONALIZATION)**	2. Remember that she needs to feel attached to all of what and who you are. Your sharing with her makes her part of your world. This makes her feel at one with you and provides a constant source of encouragement. It will help her feel secure.

TRYING LEVEL

3. Sometimes treat her as if she is overreacting to everything? Do you give her the impression that she is impossible to please or satisfy? Have you shown less willingness to try?

(BREAKDOWN)

3. Remember that she requires a warm personal relationship with you. Children are great, but they are not enough. A job is great, but it is not enough. She needs your companionship, affection, and communication. She feels lonely. Be patient and reassuring. Express your love and spend time with her doing things she enjoys doing. Make her feel needed. This is a major need that she has. She is feeling abandoned and she is having serious doubts about your love. Look at and dwell on her good points.

MEN. . .ASK YOURSELF. . .

CRYING LEVEL

DO YOU. . .	THEN SEEK TO. . .
4. Sometimes show her that nothing matters? Do you sigh a lot at her communicated expectations? Do you act as if there is no hope because she is impossible to please? **(SUFFOCATION)**	4. Remember that she is heading toward bitterness. Give her reason to be thankful. Live for her even though you don't feel like it. Even if you feel she doesn't deserve good treatment, remember that she still will respond to consistent, appreciative tenderness. Re-energize the relationship by doing fun things and knowing when to be serious. Encourage her to not quit and make sure you don't quit. Suggest Christian counseling.

CRYING LEVEL

5. Sometimes "run away" from her by working long hours, avoid intimacy because you don't like her anymore, or choose to be with others rather than her? Have you even opted for interest in other women who seem to care about you?

(ESCAPE)

5. Remember that your wife has gone from initially feeling abandoned to now feeling abused. Her reaction or lack of response is her way of acting out her lack of hope and utter disappointment in you. In order to diminish her rebellion against you, you must make immediate changes in your priorities. She needs to see obvious and sustained evidence that you care about her and the marriage. Get some professional, Christian help.

CRYING LEVEL

6. Sometimes act either like you're not going to care about anything anymore or that you are now taking total control of everything, whether she likes it or not? Are you determined that it's your turn to win? Have you become inflexible?

(ENCOUNTER)

6. Remember that your wife may be acting out of control, but she feels as if she has tried everything to get your attention. All she ever wanted was the love you both once had. She doesn't know what else to do. She is really experiencing fear as well as anger. She is ready to really emotionally quit. You can prevent this. There is hope. With good Christian counseling, you must change her perceptions of you. Show her that you are willing to be accountable to her and a counselor. Be eager, be committed, be flexible, be focused on her, be tender, and be thoughtful. Be sincere, because you are on the brink of emotional disaster. If you don't get good Christian counseling now, it could be too late.

MEN. . .ASK YOURSELF. . .

DO YOU. . .	THEN SEEK TO. . .

DYING LEVEL

7. Sometimes behave aimlessly to her indifference? Have you actually tried to do some wonderful things for her, with little or no positive response? Have you put less focus on "winning" and more focus on winning her?

(HELPLESSNESS)

7. Remember that while women go through many minor emotional withdrawals from their husbands, this could be the big ultimate one. She has so much pain from you that she is numb to you. At this point there is more fear in going back to caring than there is just to "close the door" to her heart. It is safer to release you from her life. Remember though, that she can still recover her feelings if she will allow herself to risk emotionally. Don't quit! God and a good counselor could motivate her to try. You must be a changed man in order to "sell her" on the dream of how it could be. Be consistent! Love her. . .simply love her!

DYING LEVEL

8. Sometimes or almost all of the time now behave in a heartless manner? Are you fatalistic about the marriage? Does your anger easily flare up? Are you communicating that you are the victim and that other women would be thankful to have a man like you?

(BITTERNESS)

8. Remember that your wife's indifference in her mind is the result of emotional pain that spans a lengthy amount of time. Because she is process-oriented and integrates past, present, and future continually, she sees no hope for the two of you. She only sees hope in life without you. This is not your real wife. This is a wounded, unforgiving, angry, self-preserving woman. She believes you made her this way. You have certainly played a big part. Your real wife is still there buried beneath the armor. Your bitterness will not help the situation. You must reflect the light of change. You must accept blame, change your broken methods, and look for an open, vulnerable moment to pierce her steely heart. You must become a resource of hope. Your counselor can give you practical ideas and convey God's desire to her. Pray and work hard.

MEN. . .ASK YOURSELF. . .

DO YOU. . .	THEN SEEK TO. . .

DYING LEVEL

9. Sometimes or almost all of the time just go through the motions of marriage, for the sake of others? Are your comments about marriage and her critical and depressing? Are you doing what you want to do and is she doing what she wants to do? Do you behave hopelessly?

(HOPELESSNESS)

9. Remember that she thinks you're awful, insensitive, uncaring and hopeless. At this point maybe you are, but it's never over until it's over! With God and two willing people, your marriage is still redeemable. You must both be willing to forgive, risk, change, care, and love. In spite of all the negative experiences, there have been some good memories and fun times. With good Christian counseling, this marriage, with commitment, mutual accountability, and understanding, can still be better than it ever was. It requires the two of you giving up your pride. If you continue to remain married, your

pain will still exist. If you choose to divorce, you will take your pain with you and experience more pain due to the effects of this choice. The emotional fallout of friends and family will cause you additional stress. Mutual friendships will be forced to choose and likely disintegrate. Family relationships will be forever strained. Choose to forgive! Choose to start over! Choose to love! Choose Marital Rebirth! Give each other another chance! Give yourself a chance! Give God a chance!

MARITAL DEATH INVENTORY

Introduction: Each person in a marriage has his/her own individual perceptions of the relationship. Even though your spouse may see things differently, nevertheless it is what they believe to be true. Women, after you have fully evaluated yourself ask your partner what they think about these "Marital Death" symptoms and alter his perceptions by making minor adjustments in your behavior. While you cannot personally change him, you can change yourself, thereby effecting change in his perceptions. These changed perceptions create a new reality and responsiveness.

WOMEN. . .ASK YOURSELF. . .

DO YOU. . .	THEN SEEK TO. . .

TRYING LEVEL

1. Sometimes communicate that you feel as if you are unimportant and unnecessary to your husband when he appears "zoned out" and mentally out of touch?

(APPREHENSION)

1. Remember that verbal intimacy is not as natural to him as it is for you. He tends to do it in spurts. Just because he is not totally wrapped up in you doesn't mean that he's shutting you out. His tendency to focus his thoughts elsewhere should not be taken so personally.

2. Sometimes barrage your husband with questions that require detailed answers? Do you wait for an appropriate time to talk with him? In trying to help him, do you say things that he perceives to be ego-threatening?

(DISCOURAGEMENT)

2. Remember that he often conceptually recalls information without great detail unless he is highly interested in it. Remember to give him time to unwind. Timing is often important to his willingness to communicate. Be cautious not to appear critical of his "manliness." He needs your support.

TRYING LEVEL

3. Sometimes withdraw from him and treat him "coolly" because you cannot trust his emotional commitment to you? Do you act as if there is no hope for the two of you?

(ISOLATION)

3. Remember that when he gets frustrated and feels that your behavior is extreme, he may temporarily quit trying because he thinks you are unappreciative. He is not as enduring as you when he feels abused. He is feeling undeservedly guilty. Give him continuing unconditional forgiveness, encouraging him to come out of his "compartments" without nagging. Don't assume he should understand. Warm up anyway by looking at and dwelling on his good points.

WOMEN. . .ASK YOURSELF. . .

CRYING LEVEL

DO YOU. . .	THEN SEEK TO. . .
4. Sometimes recite to him a list of his past failures that you have never forgotten? Have you trumpeted his insensitivity? Have you belittled him? Have you repeatedly announced that he'll never change, because you fear that he won't? **(BITTERNESS)**	4. Remember that because we are forgiven by God, we can and must forgive others. In order for you to help yourself, you must repeatedly and endlessly forgive your husband. You must increase your forgiveness and decrease your expectations for him to perform. This will free you from emotional and spiritual bondage and free him to begin again. Suggest Christian counseling.

CRYING LEVEL

5. Sometimes yell or scream at him? In anger, do you throw things at him, become violent, or withdraw to lengthy periods of silence? Are you now choosing to be with others rather than him? Have you even opted for interest in other men to make you feel significant and loved?

(REACTION)

5. Remember that even though you are presently feeling abused, your husband has felt abused for some time. It doesn't matter that you don't think he is, he believes he is. He feels that he has lost control of the stable foundation of his life, his marriage. He is on the verge of extremely taking control to feel like a man again. It is not going to feel good to you. You will probably not be happy with his methods. In order to avoid this, you must diffuse his hopelessness. He needs to see you care about him, show some warmth, be willing to start over, and get some professional, Christian help.

CRYING LEVEL

6. Sometimes become totally unpredictable in your reactions? Do you appear more and more indifferent? Does it seem as if you have totally given up on the marriage? Does your lack of caring frighten you? Are you afraid the marriage is finally over?

(FEAR)

6. Remember that his rigid approach to taking control, or giving it up, probably in a most undesirable way, is really a futile attempt to feel like a man again. He believes that you are in total control and constantly winning. This aggressive or passive philosophy is not only a defense mechanism to restore his pride, but also a tool of "last ditch" manipulation. He doesn't know what else to do. Remember your vows of commitment, remember the mandates of Scripture, don't listen to friends or family encouraging you to quit. If you haven't seen your pastor yet, do so now! You must have good Christian counseling now.

WOMEN. . .ASK YOURSELF. . .

DYING LEVEL

DO YOU. . .	THEN SEEK TO. . .
7. Sometimes or almost all of the time act cold to him? Do you make him feel as if you wish he didn't exist? Do you dampen his every attempt at caring, by hurtful looks, nasty tone of voice, and cutting comments? **(RELEASE)**	7. Remember that your "not caring" began with a decision to not do so, in order to protect yourself. Because it was a choice, it can change with a new choice. You can choose to love, and eventually love your choice. Yes, it requires risking, but all of life is a risk. The sizes of risks may differ, but they are all nevertheless necessary. Seek God's help. Seek to do it for Him. He loves you and wants to renew your mind and heart. A renewed marriage and a changed husband are worth the risk. Don't quit! It's always too soon to quit! Because he is fully accountable, there is hope!

DYING LEVEL

8. Sometimes or almost all of the time treat him now as if he is a non-factor in your life? Do you no longer consult with him on anything? Do you make him feel as if he is invisible? Has your anger tucked itself under hardened, protected purpose? Is everyone else now far more important than him?

(INDIFFERENCE)

8. Remember that his bitterness is a way of closing the door on his responsibility for your actions. He is isolating his thoughts. He believes that he is the victim of your overly-emotional expectations. He believes that only a perfect man could ever satisfy you. He thinks he's a good man with just a few weaknesses. He feels you have only seen the weaknesses and that you really don't deserve him, and that he certainly doesn't need you. This is not your real husband. His male ego (sensitive to begin with) is shattered because he feels that in your unswerving cold actions to be independent of him, you have trampled him into insignificance. His bitterness is but a rallying attitude to make him feel safe in a future world of uncertainty. The man you once knew is still there. His potential still exists, if you would only give him a chance. While he may not deserve another chance, you are now the one who could yet rescue the marriage. Your emotional release experience has caused you to permanently give up. Men do not deal with ultimate emotional release the same way. He could respond if given hope. Therefore, only you, at this point, could save the marriage. You could, with the counselor's help, reverse it all. Pray! Forgive! Risk!

WOMEN. . .ASK YOURSELF. . .

DYING LEVEL

DO YOU. . .	THEN SEEK TO. . .
9. Sometimes or almost all of the time just go through the motions of marriage, for the sake of others? Are your comments about marriage and him critical and depressing? Are you doing what you want to do and is he doing what he wants to do? Do you behave hopelessly? **(HOPELESSNESS)**	9. Remember that he thinks you're awful, insensitive, uncaring and hopeless. At this point maybe you are, but it's never over until it's over! With God and two willing people, your marriage is still redeemable. You must both be willing to forgive, risk, change, care, and love. In spite of all the negative experiences, there have been some good memories and fun times. With good Christian counseling this marriage, with commitment, mutual accountability, and understanding can still be better than it ever was. It requires the two of you giving up your pride. If you continue to remain married, your pain will still exist. If you choose to divorce, you will take your pain with you and experience more pain due to the effects of this choice.

The emotional fallout of friends and family will cause you additional stress. Mutual friendships will be forced to choose and likely disintegrate. Family relationships will be forever strained. Choose to forgive! Choose to start over! Choose to love! Choose Marital Rebirth! Give each other another chance! Give yourself a chance! Give God a chance!

"O Lord my God, if I have done this,

if there be iniquity in my hands,

If I have rewarded evil unto him who

was at peace with me (yea, I have

delivered him who without cause is mine

enemy),

Let the enemy persecute my soul, and

take it; yea, let him tread down my life

upon the earth, and lay mine HONOR

IN THE DUST."

Psalm 7:3-5

"MARITAL DEATH"

All things. . .bright and beautiful. . .

    Everything going so well. . .

        A marriage. . .made in heaven. . .

            A perfected place. . .to dwell. . .

Unsettled. . .lonely feelings. . .

    An erosion. . .of what was. . .

        Too hard. . .to identify. . .

            Just rejection. . .without a cause. . .

Everything. . .going so wrong. . .

    How could this happen. . .to us?

        Love and respect. . .used to count. . .

            All honor. . .lies in the dust. . .

Hard to believe. . .it's over. . .

    Wasn't like this. . . when we wed..

        Not sure. . .just how it happened. . .

            All that I know. . .is. . .it's dead. . .

    Marital Death. . .

Richard R. George

CHAPTER THREE

"HOPE!"

This is the story of the Battle of Franklin, Tennessee, as told by that great evangelist of the past, Sam Jones.

"I don't like to bring up memories of the late war, but this one which I heard will serve as an example of what I am going to say. When Johnston turned over his army to Hood at Atlanta, he placed it in the care of a great man. Hood was a brave man, and when he came around to Tennessee, the great battle of Franklin, of which you all have heard, took place. Hood's tent was stationed on an eminence, and as he walked around near the tent he could see a fort, in a locust grove, literally mowing down his ranks. He was moved to tears at the sight, and calling his adjutant-general, said: "Present my compliments to Gen. Cheatham, and tell him to take that fort in the locust grove." The adjutant started off, and soon returned, telling his general that Gen. Cheatham was missing and supposed to be dead. The tears trickled down the cheeks of the brave general, but whenever he turned he saw that fort in the locust grove literally tearing his army to pieces. He again called his adjutant, and instructed him to present his compliments to Gen. Cleburne, and tell him to take the fort, but the adjutant soon returned with the intelligence that the general was dead on the field. Gen. Hood again looked sorrowfully toward the locust grove and saw the fort literally tearing his army to pieces, and again calling his adjutant he said, "Present my love to Gen. Cockrell and ask him to take that fort for me." When Gen. Cockrell got the order he shouted: "Come on, first Missouri regiment, and take that fort." They responded and the fort was soon taken.

Sam Jones went on to explain the relevance of the story. "I am here as the Lord's adjutant-general. He calls upon me to have you conquer the evil of this city just like that fort and bring about its redemption and I want you to take this city to God. Work will have to be done, and only by strong fighting can this city be redeemed."

Now Sam Jones, in telling the story, was not commenting on the people of the southern city. In fact, I'm confident that those southern soldiers believed they were being attacked by evil forces. Each had their own perception of reality.

The point of the story is found in the last line. "Work will have to be done, and only by strong fighting can this city be redeemed." The last thing you heard in the last chapter was "Choose to forgive! Choose to start over! Work will have to be done! Choose to love! Fight hard! Choose Marital Rebirth! Your marriage can be redeemed. Give each other another chance."

Give yourself a chance! Give God a chance! I have asked you, implored you, challenged you, beseeched you, and yes I have even begged you!

Many years ago, when I was a teacher, my heart had grown hard and insensitive toward my wife, Susan. The same thing had happened to her, in terms of her feelings toward me. We had a two year old son named Jamie. We loved him deeply, but had come to a place where our love for ourselves even exceeded the great love we had for him.

While we had received competent Christian counseling, we were "self-will run riot" in terms of our own personal desire for happiness. While the counseling should have worked, it didn't. We actually understood some of the things you just read about in the general remedy for "Marital Death."

Our families begged us to succeed, our friends prayed, our church sought to help, our pastor did all he could, but our self-absorbed hearts were fixed on another path.

I still remember clearly the day of our "last" appointment with the highly-trained pastor. Sue and I had gone to lunch, where we both agreed that there was no longer any hope for the marriage. After all, how could there be any hope when we felt as if we didn't love each other, didn't like each other, didn't want each other, and couldn't even stand touching each other? It was over. The skillful and well-intended pastor didn't yet know, that we had decided that this was without question or persuasion, our last counseling session.

We finished our lunch and hurried to the church, as to not be late. The only thing on our minds, besides our determined and irrevocable decision, was the distaste we had for disappointing the pastor for whom we had great affection. We weren't contemplating much of what God thought about it. I'm sure we knew and I'm sure we didn't care.

Just like General Cheatham and General Cleburne at the battle of Franklin, we were already defeated and already dead (maritally speaking). Then there was a surprise twist upon our arrival. The pastor (who didn't know about our irreversible decision) had always counseled us together, but not that day. He asked to see Sue first, while I waited outside in the outer office with a crusty, yet efficient secretary and my swirling, mind-numbing thoughts. I remember that I didn't like this new tactic of taking her and leaving me outside. I hoped that he didn't think things were going to change because of that. We had made our decision and it was final.

At least that's what I thought. Little did I suspect that in the next few moments my life was going to dramatically change forever. As I picked up a magazine and began to aimlessly look for something of interest, I received a rare privilege that I did not deserve or want. I heard the voice of God.

I know! I know! There are a lot of people who say that and we sometimes wonder how much of that is true, especially since God doesn't typically speak out loud to His people on a regular basis anymore. But I know that I heard God speak to me. It wasn't audible, with my ears. I wish I could say that it was the still small voice of God, but it wasn't exactly like that either.

It was in my head, and maybe somehow in my soul and spirit. I could never accurately describe the how, but I sure did know it was Him. He told me, "I don't want you to do this." (I hope you're sitting down when you read this.) I said, "God you don't understand!" You heard me. I actually was so hard-hearted and so foolish that I thought that the God of the universe (and then some) who created everything, by just speaking it into existence, did not understand. What was I thinking? I praise God He didn't kill me on the spot for insulting Him. I told Him, "I don't love her, I don't like her, and I don't want her." He said, "I know, but that doesn't matter now. I don't want you to divorce her. I will help you." To which I responded, "But God, if I feel as if I don't love her, like her, or want her, how can I feel differently? It just seems easier to end it all and start over." God said, "I want you to choose to love her." (I must confess that I didn't think that His answer sounded very God-like. A miraculous and instant change in my feelings seemed more appropriate. In fact, it sounded like a lot of hard work and unselfish sacrifice, which I did not want to do.) I remember saying, "But

God, if I don't even want her, why would I choose to love her?" He then put things in the perspective He wanted me to grasp. He said, "If you choose to love her, I will give you the want to and I will restore your love feelings." In essence, He was saying, "Choose to love and love your choice."

That was it. That's all He said. That's all He needed to say. In the midst of immediately realizing that this was not "self-talk" but an order from God, my heart melted and I repented of my wrongful attitude, lack of faith, disobedient spirit, and self-obsessed thinking.

Almost immediately, (or so it seemed), the pastor's office door opened and he invited me in, with a bewildered expression on his face, as he looked at my unexpected countenance.

Sue was sitting in the far chair, away from the door and in front of the desk. She seemed as if she had been crying. He invited me to sit down in the chair nearest the door and next to Sue, as he sat down behind his desk. While I'm sure he was intending to say something potentially persuasive, I didn't give him the chance.

I blurted out the account about my "just a few moments ago" experience in the outer office, and that I had dramatically changed my mind. I emotionally told Sue that I really wanted to make the marriage work. I asked her if she was willing also. She replied emotionally as well, responding that she was willing. It seemed as if she was more nodding than speaking.

I don't know what happened next. My mind was a blur. I had just had an encounter with the one and only living God, and our marriage got a new lease on life at the same time. What a life-shaking paradigm shift, to say the least.

It was a new commitment for both of us. It wasn't easy, but it was worth it. Because of our selfishness (mostly mine), it took longer than it should have. I was the poster boy for selfish, stubborn, and slow to change. But as we both became more sacrificial, we became more pleasing to God. The closer we got to the Lord, the more sacrificial we became.

God had a mighty plan to rescue my marriage and my family. Beyond that, He had even bigger plans. We have four children today, all loving and serving God. My son Jamie (with his wonderful wife), pastors a cutting-edge church in Franklin, Tennessee and my three special girls (Jodi, Jineen, and Joy) that followed him have all married wonderful like-minded Christian men, also serving God. Sue and I were called into full-time ministry where God has used us beyond our comprehensions for almost 35 years.

While "growing up" and growing more and more in love with my wife, God and Sue taught me how women think (a rare and unique understanding most men do not have, even male counselors). I am blessed and humbled to be able to effectively help singles, husbands and wives, the newly engaged, and even teenagers understand one another, as they never have before.

Today (just like General Hood), God looks down from His place of eminence, knowing that He personally sent His power and love in a General Cockrell-like fashion and the fortress of our pride and unyielding obstinence was defeated and occupied by the passionate forces of sacrifice, commitment, and togetherness.

Friend, let me remind you of the last line of Sam Jones' story again. "Work will have to be done, and only by strong fighting can this city be redeemed."

There are many broken-down, or poorly constructed fortresses of marriage today, in many cities and places all around this world. They are steadfastly and ferociously opposing everything and anything that can redeem them.

Pride rules the day and stubbornness rules the night. Each partner waiting for the other to change, rejects and repels the attempts of God to bring real freedom, safety, and significance, even coldly mowing down the real answers to their overwhelming crisis.

They may have even half-heartedly or sincerely cracked open the highly fortified doors of their hearts to the "Marital Death" process of charted hope, but gave up due to residual belligerence and questionable commitment.

That is precisely why the "Marital Life" remedy was created; to provide a more detailed and exhaustive understanding to two ready and willing hearts. Your marriage really can live again, beyond any previous experience. It can be deeper and wider. The plan is simple, but the work is hard, yet worth it. It goes right back to what God told me. "Choose to live for the other. He will give you the want to and restore the love." Your behavior will change your attitude and your attitude will then maintain your behaviors, and then the feelings will follow.

It's one thing to fight each other, but imagine your strength, determination, faith, and sacrifice fighting together on the same team for a victorious marriage and formidable family. Work will have to be done, and only by strong fighting can your city (married life) be redeemed.

"MARITAL LIFE"

Most things. . .bright and beautiful. . .

    It's finally going well. . .

        Hard work. . .and help from heaven. . .

            Have made a great place. . .to dwell. . .

Forgiveness. . .renewed feelings. . .

    Thankfulness. . .of what was. . .

        Not hard. . .to identify. . .

            Humility. . .shows the cause. . .

All the things. . .that went so wrong. . .

    Were bound to happen. . .to us. . .

        We never knew. . .what did count. . .

            So our love. . .just gathered dust. . .

The battles now. . .are over. . .

    It's better now. . .then when wed. . .

        It's great. . .how real love's happened. . .

            Now Marital. . .Death. . .is dead. . .

    Marital Life. . .

Richard R. George

Story 1.

Many years ago I saw an attractive young couple in big trouble. Roy was a civil servant. He had lots of exposure to lots of people, especially women. He was married and the children were young. His wife Jennifer was an attractive young woman who was proud of her husband, her children and her husband's work.

Being flirtatious (which he was known for), good-looking and making himself appear "available," finally got him trapped in an affair, which was difficult to hide in a small town.

They had recently begun coming to our church and having found out about her husband's infidelity, Jennifer came to me in tears. She didn't want to lose her husband. She was embarrassed, distraught, and hopeless. She asked if I would call him, since I had known him for awhile. Roy came in and admitted everything. He was contrite and ashamed. He knew his pride, his looks, his personality, and his position were a detriment to living a life for his wife, his kids, and his God.

We began steady and consistent counseling. In those days there was no "Marital Death" or "Marital Life" Chart, because I hadn't figured it all out yet. With God's help and continuous loving biblical counsel, they finally put the past behind them and chose to risk, hope, trust, believe, forgive, and forget (at least where the memories were not actively interfering with their everyday lives).

For a great number of years they have been pillars of integrity and shining examples to acquaintances, friends, family and specifically their children. Thank God for their ultimate painstaking success.

Because there was no progressive protocol to understand or follow, the restoration of their marriage probably took at least a year.

Story 2.

It was another Christian man. Surely it must be God's will! That is what Alicia had convinced herself, when she was planning on divorcing her husband Alex. Marriage had become boring and predictable for her. Alex was either physically out of town or emotionally out of touch for some time. Yes, they were both religious and even considered themselves "followers of Christ." They served in church (but not together) and believed emphatically in marriage as a holy and irreversible union.

That was until Alicia one day met a very nice man who seemed to be very courteous, conscientious, and considerate of her. After meeting together "as friends" on several occasions, the relationship began to deepen into an emotional affair. She was emotionally divorced from her husband and convinced she was in love with this man. After all, he claimed to believe in God the same way she did. Maybe this was in fact meant to be. Maybe God brought him along to rescue her from her unsatisfied and unfulfilled marriage of pain and rejection. Yes, that was it. This third person was clearly sent by God. After all, didn't God want us to be happy? She clearly wasn't happy, so God was rescuing her.

It was at this point that she just couldn't contain herself and she told Alex, who was devastated. Frustrated, fearful, and not knowing what to do, Alex called me. He asked if I would see them, even though she was highly reluctant to come. She wasn't planning on changing her mind. God wanted her to be happy and happy was what she was going to be.

Alicia finally relented and I began to see them both together. Clearly Alex had neglected her and made her vulnerable to an affair. Clearly she chose to give in to that vulnerability and even convinced herself that it was God's will.

After a couple months of consistent counseling, she began to realize that if God created marriage, hates divorce, and only gives opportunity for it when there is ongoing sexual immortality and/or desertion by an unbeliever, she really didn't have God's endorsement for dissolving the marriage. In order for her scenario of "happiness" to become a reality, she clearly had to violate biblical principles, which God could not condone, since He put them in place.

Alex (having personal issues of his own) began placing his priorities in all the right places. With his new awareness, in meekness he forgave and even thanked God for the bad, so he could make it all good. His focus, attentiveness, and his willingness to unselfishly share of himself for Alicia helped her to respond. His patience, consistency, and dedication helped her to forget about the marital invader and she began to love Alex again.

Because Alicia was willing to please God, recognizing her need for His help, she humbly also took on an attitude of thankfulness that there could be a "beginning again," which also helped her to forgive Alex for ignoring her needs. She began to behaviorally, attitudinally, and emotionally risk and as a result began to hope in him and finally respond to him. Her emotional trust began to increase in him, while decreasing in the third party, who was now long gone from the scene. Her faith in God grew and the smiles on her face increased as her devotion to God, her husband, and her marriage reached new heights.

The following Marital Life Chart will help you observe the progress of Alex and Alicia.

Story 3.

Mike had been "fooling around" being unfaithful to his trusting and loving wife, Diane. They'd only been married about 18 months and were both working hard to improve their quality of life. Diane tells the story this way: "After getting married, earning a Master's degree, and buying a home, I felt as though something in my life was missing. I did not feel complete. A friend asked me to attend church with her. During the sermon, I found what I was missing in my life.

Jesus! That day I accepted Jesus as my personal savior and would turn my life over to Him. My husband had attended the service with me, but stated "It's not for me."

For a year I attended church every Sunday by myself. I prayed each day for my husband and his salvation. Eleven months later I realized that my marriage was falling apart. My husband started acting different. He didn't seem to be himself. He was angry and many things seemed to bother him. At this time I couldn't stand to be around him. I stopped praying for my husband and began to distance myself from God. My marriage was a mess, I wasn't happy, and I felt as though I was completely alone. Mike and I began to communicate less, spend less time with one another, and worst of all (rather than growing together), we grew apart.

One Monday night, on my way to a women's Bible study in November, I pulled over my car because I felt the urge to pray. I had a feeling my husband was being unfaithful. I had asked God to give me guidance. If my husband was cheating, I wanted to know. That same week on Wednesday, my worst nightmare came true. I found out he had indeed been unfaithful. Not knowing what to do, I just hit my knees, cried, and poured my heart out to God. I thought my marriage was over. I was ready to start looking for a new apartment, pack my bags, and leave my husband.

On Thursday I spoke (by telephone) to my husband for the very first time since I found out, as I had moved in with my mom. I was screaming, yelling, and saying some awful things.

My husband then said to me, "I went to The Chapel today, and as I sat there, I remembered all the times you asked me to come with you and I didn't go. I wished you were there with me today. I realize now that God is my only hope for my marriage."

That next Sunday was the first time I had seen Mike since the incident; he sat behind me at church. That day he was saved. I walked into the bookstore and purchase my husband his first bible. In it I wrote, "Ask and you will be forgiven. To my husband from your wife."

Mike and I began counseling immediately and have been working on our marriage ever since. The marriage we have today compares nothing to the marriage we had. God has broken our hearts, but he has also healed us. It was not long after the incident that Mike and I were given hope. Our very first counseling session, Pastor George convinced me and showed me how to forgive Mike, understanding that I also had done wrong. He explained that just like God has forgiven me, I needed to forgive Mike. I not only forgave my husband, but also forgive the "other girl." Mike additionally was contrite and began to show consistent loving effort. Immediately I began to heal.

Since this painful incident, Mike and I have grown together. We pray each night, we pray each morning, we attend church together regularly and volunteer within our church community. God has really turned our lives around. God has healed us and given us something so unbelievable. We continue to work on our issues and grow together, applying the "Marital Life" principles of success. Mike and I are so thankful for the marriage we have today. Had we not found God and wisely followed biblical counsel after a year and a half of marriage, we would have been just another statistic added to the divorce rate.

Mike and Diane are a couple that moved quickly and anxiously from "Dealing"(Level I of Marital Life Chart) to "Kneeling" (Level II), to "Feeling" (Level III), to "Healing" (Level IV) within a very short period of time. Their marriage was a catastrophe and they had to relearn almost everything, but with God's help, their faithfulness to Him, one another, and my counsel, they remain sparkling marital models for all to follow (and people are following).

CHAPTER FOUR

"MARITAL LIFE!"
(RECONSTRUCTION BY CHOICE)

"MAN"				"WOMAN"			
LEVEL I "DEALING"	**PHASE PROCESS** AWARENESS	PRAYER	"GOD, THANK YOU FOR ANOTHER CHANCE!"	**PERCEPTION** "I UNDERSTAND MY PART IN OUR FAILURE: I MUST TRY TO LIVE FOR HER."	**PHASE PROCESS** WILLINGNESS	PRAYER	"GOD, I AM AFRAID, HELP US SUCCEED?"	**PERCEPTION** "IN SPITE OF MY FEELINGS, I REALLY WANT TO DO THE RIGHT THING."
LEVEL II "KNEELING"	MEEKNESS FORGIVENESS THANKFULNESS	PRAYER	"LORD, HELP ME BE A GODLY MAN?"	"I MUST ASSUME MY RESPONSIBILITES" "FORGIVENESS FREES ME!" "GOD HAS ALLOWED THIS TO MAKE ME MORE LIKE HIM."	HUMILITY THANKFULNESS FORGIVENESS	PRAYER	"LORD, HELP ME OVERCOME MY WOUNDS?"	"I MUST SACRIFICE MY RIGHTS AND PRIDE." "BE THANKFUL IN SPITE OF MY FEELINGS" "I'M COMMANDED TO FORGIVE AGAIN AND AGAIN!"
LEVEL III "FEELING"	FOCUS ATTENTIVENESS SHARING	PRAYER	"GOD, I FEEL LIKE I CARE. THANK YOU."	"SHE NEEDS TO BE REASSURED OF MY LOVE." "I MUST PAY ATTENTION TO LITTLE THINGS." "IS SHE GETTING ENOUGH VERBAL INTIMACY?"	RISK HOPE RESPONSE	PRAYER	"GOD, HELP HIM TO NOT QUIT. MY FEELINGS ARE COMING BACK."	"I MUST SOMEHOW GIVE HIM A CHANCE." "I CAN'T BELIEVE HE THOUGHT OF DOING THAT." "AM I MAKING HIM FEEL LIKE A MAN?"
LEVEL IV "HEALING"	PATIENCE CONSISTENCY DEDICATION	PRAYER	"THANK YOU GOD FOR THIS WONDERFUL WOMAN!"	"I SEE THE VALUE OF SHARING FEELINGS." "I CANNOT QUIT! I DARE NOT QUIT!" "SHE LOVES ME AND REALLY DOES COMPLETE ME!"	TRUST FAITH DEVOTION	PRAYER	"THANK YOU GOD FOR THIS AMAZING MAN!"	"I FEEL MUCH SAFER!" "I REALLY DO BELIEVE IN HIM!" "HE REALLY LOVES ME! I FEEL SO MYUCH A PART OF HIM!"

MARITAL LIFE

"I know what the Bible says, but it would be easier to start over with someone else!" These are typical words couples in the descending process of "Marital Death," have uttered in "emotional divorce."

The MARITAL LIFE Chart is an ascending and progressive tool of life-changing benchmarks, that through timely and competent Christian Counseling (or possibly even without) the counselees will DEAL with the issues, KNEEL to their Christian responsibilities, FEEL marital love again, and HEAL their broken and battered marriages.

This "reconstruction by choice" is possible because the human central nervous system is designed by God to most readily respond to behavioral change. Therefore we all can choose to love, and love our choice.

By using biblical principles of loving behavior, understanding, and mutual accountability, hope and help is on the way:

LEVEL I (DEALING)

In the AWARENESS phase, the husband recognizes how his "compartmentalized thinking" neglected his wife. He wants a real chance. In WILLINGNESS the wife sees that her "Chainlink-thinking" cultivated assumptions on her part and misunderstanding on his. She has motivation to begin again.

LEVEL II (KNEELING)

In MEEKNESS his attitude makes him willing to be responsible for his actions. In HUMILITY her actions reflect her surrender of pride.

In FORGIVENESS he forfeits his "power" over her and releases himself from bondage. In THANKFULNESS she obeys God with her attitude, probably not totally with her heart yet.

In THANKFULNESS he acknowledges that God is working His plan. In FORGIVENESS she anticipates prolonged and positive change.

LEVEL III (FEELING)

In FOCUS he returns to the loving behaviors, communication, and protective accountability that once spontaneously evoked love. In RISK, she silently applauds his efforts and with guarded reservation slowly unlocks emotional barricades.

In ATTENTIVENESS he gives evidence of "living for her." In HOPE she softens her heart as she sees his sincerity.

In SHARING information, feelings, and thoughts, he makes her "feel loved." In RESPONSE her defenses "come down" and she begins to respect him again.

LEVEL IV (HEALING)

In PATIENCE he "stays the course" of meeting newly understood needs. In TRUST, she no longer lets her pain control her.

In CONSISTENCY, he fights his "Compartmentalized-thinking" tendencies to forget her relational needs and perseveres in doing the "little things." In FAITH, her "built in responder" motivates her to "out-give" him.

In DEDICATION, he cherishes her more than ever. He abides in her. In DEVOTION, she feels so connected, that she treasures him. She abides in him.

MARITAL LIFE INVENTORY

Introduction: Each person in a marriage has his/her own individual perceptions of the relationship. Even though your spouse may see things differently, nevertheless it is what they believe to be true. Men, after you have fully evaluated yourself, ask your partner what they think about these "Marital Life" evidences and discuss how they are effectively influencing their thinking.

Remember that you cannot personally "wave a magic wand" and change her, but you can steadily alter her perceptions by making positive and consistent communicated strides in your behaviors and attitudes.

Always remember to speak the truth out of an ocean of love, to best facilitate open and honest dialogue. Be mindful that "it's always too soon to quit," and that even the smallest positive changes that you make can produce great hope and change of perceptions on the part of your spouse. These changed perceptions create a new reality and refreshed responsiveness.

MEN. . .ASK YOURSELF. . .

DO YOU. . .	THEN SEEK TO. . .

KNEELING LEVEL

1. Realize that most men have a tendency to be selfish, stubborn, and slow to change? Because you get most of your esteem from your job and /or hobbies, it is easier for you to enjoy tasks that please you, rather than her. You need to be admired and respected to feel like a "man." Your wife was not created to be like you. Because she is driven by relationship, you will often feel "pressured" to meet her needs. She is easily disappointed because she is usually accustomed to sacrifice for you and thinks that it should be just as easy for you to sacrifice for her. Her natural ability to "chain link" her thoughts helps her, while your "compartmentalizing" hinders you, when it comes to intimate relationship.

1. Take responsibility. It's a great beginning. Remember that a woman needs to know that she is loved. Telling her is important, but showing her is imperative. You do that best by sacrificially living to please her. Only by serving her often will she know you are serious about loving her and only then will her heart begin to warm and hope begin to grow. This sacrifice on your part is a spiritual issue. The Bible clearly indicates that an attitude of service and responsibility does not make you weak, but instills, activates, and evidences admirable and noticeable strength. This may appear to be the wrong road to take, but is similar to the one you took when you first fell in love and it worked.

(MEEKNESS)

MEN. . .ASK YOUR SELF. . .

DO YOU. . .	THEN SEEK TO. . .

KNEELING LEVEL

2. Know that men tend to be far more conditional in how we act toward our wives? There may be things that have bothered you for a long time. It could be her family, her size, being late, how she dresses, how she reacts to you, etc. All of your complaining, criticizing, or conditional love has not changed any of it. It usually doesn't. Remember that "servanthood" mentioned in the previous phase? But who wants to serve when the other person isn't pleasing you? When they don't please you, it's easier to "hold back" or "hold it in," therefore sort of acting distant and not forgiving her. Believe it or not, forgiveness gives control to God and strips you of excessive

2. Forgive her! Stop trying to change her. Keep forgiving her and live for her. This feels backwards and easier for you to be motivated to forgive if she changed. It actually works just the opposite. Women put such priority on being loved, that by loving unconditionally, they are more motivated to please you when they feel totally accepted by you. Women find great security in acceptance and great significance when they are loved. Do what doesn't feel right and thank God for her. Whether it's her overreactions, her craziness, her emotional outbursts, her coldness, or whatever. Be thankful you have another chance at getting this right. Ask God for help. Pray! Maybe she doesn't deserve forgiveness. So what,

judgmental power that condemns her, because she isn't perfect, or exactly the way you want her. In fact, your unforgiveness has greatly hampered this relationship and impaired her desire to please you. God probably hasn't been much pleased with you either.

neither do you. Unforgiveness is like a long, thick, heavy chain forged by your pride (which is also a sin) that holds you back, blackens your soul, and robs you of peace and joy. Forgive her and enjoy the freedom as the slave-chains of condemnation fall away and you begin to see her beauty again.

(FORGIVENESS)

MEN. . .ASK YOURSELF. . .

DO YOU. . .	THEN SEEK TO. . .

KNEELING LEVEL

3. Recognize that your attitude has greatly shaped your actions in the past, and that by having a new and different attitude; it can shape your actions in the future. There are "no accidents," only incidents that can influence and control the purposes of your life. An appreciative attitude is a choice. You will be greatly tested here. You have a great opportunity to lead and "show the way." Never forget that God is in charge and that He knows everything, including your circumstances and your feelings. Don't blame Him for your inability to love your wife correctly. Put Him in the middle of this and at the end, because He has a better plan than you can possibly imagine.

3. Do whatever it takes. Be a man and lead like you've never chosen to lead before. Turn a "scar into a star." Think thanks! Make a list of 7-10 items (even if it's small things) you like about her and thank god for each item on this list at least 3 times a day. Determine to not criticize or complain. Try not to be negative or yell, using a loud "father" voice. Notice positive things and compliment her on them. This approach will help you appreciate her all the more and serve to additionally motivate you. The more you use this approach, the quicker your heart will begin to stir again. Though this feels "wrong," it is the only way back. If God is preparing us for heaven, then the world in which we live is not only "a vapor that appears for a time and

Now that He has your full attention, He will help you if you take these steps of restoration. He loves you and He just wants you to "step up to the plate" and engage this promised relationship with total trust and integrity.

then passes away," but a basic-training battleground, used by God to shape us and prepare us for an everlasting life in eternity. Therefore, thank God in everything!

(THANKFULNESS)

MEN. . .ASK YOURSELF. . .

DO YOU. . .	THEN SEEK TO. . .
4. Notice some of your old ways that tend to sneak up on you? Do you sometimes feel indifferent to your wife's needs? Have you caught yourself not paying attention to what she says? Has she commented or cried about how she doesn't think you can ever really change? Has she expressed worry and fear over your insensitivity or your not making her feel like she's a priority? When you "drift" on being a good husband, be aware that it has more to do with re-habituating doing the things that worked early on, than with the fact that you don't care. You got in negative and unproductive "ruts" that can be changed.	4. Make her your top priority. Communicate! Communicate! Communicate! Don't just talk to her, but be sure you are listening to her. Be interested in her daily activities and her conversations. Ask questions, which show a sincere interest. Find time to be alone with her, to talk face to face, so she can feel close to you. Share your life stories with her. If you don't risk now, it may be too late later. Any possible previous indiscretions by either of you should not be discussed in detail, and avoided if possible. You cannot afford to revisit the past and open old wounds. Keep it positive and enjoyable. Speak of a hopeful future while focusing on the present, having learned from the past.

FEELING LEVEL

Be sensitive to her pain from the past. Don't just tell her to "get over it." She has to process changes in you, by being reassured, not reprimanded. Don't forget to pray.

(FOCUS)

MEN. . .ASK YOURSELF. . .

DO YOU. . .	THEN SEEK TO. . .

FEELING LEVEL

5. Remember at all, how life was with her at the beginning? You may think that it was a long time ago, and she doesn't respond like that anymore. She doesn't respond because she can't As you ignored her needs or even said or did things she thought were abusive, you caused her so much pain that you sucked the ability to respond right out of her. Her spirit, which once was vulnerable and open to you, began to close up, like the fingers on an open hand begin to close and become a fist. She became tough, uncaring, caustic, and possibly even nasty. It was how she protected herself from further pain. Even silence can be deafening, so be cautious. As the emotional protector of her family, she is deeply fragile like a delicate flower, though hardly resembling one at times.

5. Reopen her spirit. Let your concern for her outweigh the concern you have for yourself. There is an old saying, "That you can never out-give God." Truer words have hardly ever been spoken. But, just as you cannot out-give God, you can never out-give a woman. Somewhere in every woman there is a secretly located, built in "responder." As you show her attentiveness, by asking her opinion, seeking to be romantic, revisiting fun things to do, and continually looking for ways to include her in your life, her spirit will begin to tremble. She will hope that just maybe, maybe you really are sincere and just maybe, this marriage really might be rekindled. Don't quit! She's afraid you will. She may even test you to see if you will. Of course she shouldn't, but she often does. Stay the course for her, for your family, for you, and for God.

(ATTENTIVENESS)

MEN. . .ASK YOURSELF. . .

DO YOU. . .	THEN SEEK TO. . .

FEELING LEVEL

6. Try to protect her from potentially bad news? Are you unwilling to talk about your work day? Do you respond to her questions by using the least number of words necessary? Do you have wonderful ideas and thoughts that you do not tell her because you think she is not interested? Do you excuse your lack of communication by saying that you just don't talk a lot and never have? Has she discovered that you only tell her half-truths or even lie? Do you find her acting coolly toward you and can't figure out why? Stop playing the "that's just the way I am" card. It is the way you have chosen to be for a long, long time. This is not about heredity; it is about choices. As long as you have a thought and have the ability to communicate that thought, you can and must do so. Choose caring and thoughtful

6. Understand that caring communication for most women is not a choice, but an absolute need. The average woman speaks at least twice as many words as a man, everyday. (Occasionally she might marry a man who out-talks her, but the great male talkers tend to be a bit self-centered and very poor listeners.) Being the emotional protector of her family requires knowledge and information exchange. While you get most of your esteem through admiration and respect (manhood), she receives hers from feeling loved. In order for her to feel loved, she needs to feel as if she matters to you. She needs to feel close to you, so she can feel secure and significant. Most women require "verbal intimacy," which means they like to get "inside your head." This helps them know what you think, feel, plan, hope, fear, and believe. It establishes emotional

methodology in doing so. Most women cannot handle direct and insensitive statements. They need a soft and kind approach. It is how they have communicated with other women all of their lives. If they did otherwise, they wouldn't have many female friends.

trust. The more she can trust your sensitive and caring honesty, the closer she feels. The closer she feels, the closer she wants to be. The closer she wants to be, leads to a desire for lovemaking, and now physical intimacy. This is ultimate closeness. To a woman, caring is evidenced by sharing.

(SHARING)`

MEN. . .ASK YOURSELF. . .

DO YOU. . .	THEN SEEK TO. . .

HEALING LEVEL

7. Really know what her needs are anymore? Have you noticed how her spirit is beginning slowly to open up? You have witnessed the value of your opening up and being vulnerable. Be steadfast in uncovering the layers of who she really is. You are in for some delightful surprises. She will often ask you many questions. She will even ask you questions about things you've never thought about. This will try your patience. You might have the tendency to be "clipped" or "short" with your answers, widening agitation. You've come too far to give in to your seeming to be insensitive again. Kindly be tolerant and tell her nicely, if you don't know the answer. Humor is very helpful here.

7. Find out what her longingss are today. Don't act on what you thought they once were, because you already failed in that arena. Besides, people go through different seasons of life. If you ever really did know what her needs were, there's a strong possibility that they are no longer the same. There are many books available today to discover her needs, as well as your own. But with or without resources, you will find out a great deal about her by asking her. It's not like you have never asked her before. This time you have a focused attentiveness that begs her to share them with you, as if she is opening a treasure chest you have long, long anticipated. If you are willing to take time in a quiet and restive setting, where there are no distractions, the blossom of her heart, previously closed, will openly

yield to the warmth of your rejuvenated and persistent tender care. This is a good time to ask her what she needs from you (pay close attention). Ask her about her need to be needed, or being appreciated, receiving compassion, feeling secure, affection, closeness, and romance. This will open up many doors and give you many ideas. You must follow through. If you don't know how, ask her. She will tell you. If you are afraid you'll forget it, write it down. This will help you immensely, due to forgetful compartmentalizing. That's why it's good to do this in a private "away" kind of place, where you can give her the proper time.

(PATIENCE)

MEN. . .ASK YOURSELF. . .

DO YOU. . .	THEN SEEK TO. . .

HEALING LEVEL

8. Get caught up in other things? Does your mind innocently wander away from your wife, particularly when working or enjoying a favorite hobby or two? Relax! You are a normal man. You tend to become compartmentalized, as you jump from what matters at this moment, to what matters in the next. Unfortunately, while this wonderfully enables you to "lock in" and focus as the "physical protector" of your family, it often leaves you dreadfully lacking in remembering relational information and specifically meeting your wife's longings.

8. Remember, that just as you tend to isolate and forget about her needs, she will integrate and never forget (or hardly ever) about yours. As a chain-linker who lives in the past, present, and future (all at the same time), she maintains a vast relational data bank, which rarely makes her wrong. She will sometimes unfairly forget that you are a compartmentalizing man and expect you to remember all of her needs. Kindly remind her that you are working very hard at relating to her "chainlink thinking" and you would hope that she is doing the same thing, when it comes to your "compartmentalizing." Become adept at sincerely asking forgiveness and ask her to help you habituate new remembrances or evidences of her longings. Ask her to be patient as you

try to get into her thinking mode of information connection. Your continuous vigilance at being sensitive to her needs will bring great reward, as she sees your remarkable efforts.

(CONSISTENCY)

MEN. . .ASK YOURSELF. . .

DO YOU. . . | THEN SEEK TO. . .

HEALING LEVEL

9. Wonder if you are becoming a "wimp?" Do you suspect that you're going way overboard to prove your love? That's normal! The real issue is not that you are forcibly giving up control, you are actually doing what you promised you'd do when you married her. You are loving her by your attitude, your actions, and your feelings. A woman needs far more than food, shelter, clothing, and physical security. Her grandmother and maybe even her mother settled for that, but if they did, they were cheated. Only by loving her sacrificially can she be the woman you fell in love with. As you love her that way, she will respond, and she will complete you more than ever.

9. Promote continuous healing. Keep doing what's working. You are honoring her, loving her, and serving her. You are protecting her emotionally from the temptations and attacks of this world. You have shown her that you are totally committed to her. She has opened her spirit and heart, once again, to the man she loved and married. Her soul is beginning to sing again. She believes in you. She trusts you. She now out-gives you. You are again her choice, her knight, her lover, her protector, and her champion. You have worked hard to get here. But you have not "arrived." This relationship will need constant vigilance, using all the things that have worked. Being a compartmentalizer, you will have a tendency to believe that the journey is over, but you are wrong. The journey has just begun. And because

you have traveled the path successfully now, you are no longer lost. You know the way. Be sure to stay on it and never quit. Now you have the tools and the know-how. Now and forevermore, enjoy the journey.

(DEDICATION)

MARITAL LIFE INVENTORY

Introduction: Each person in a marriage has his/her own individual perceptions of the relationship. Even though your partner may see things differently, nevertheless it is what they believe to be true. Women, after you have fully evaluated yourself, ask your partner what they think about these "Marital Life" evidences and discuss how they are effectively influencing their thinking.

Remember that you cannot personally "wave a magic wand" and change him, but you can alter his perceptions, by making positive and communicated strides in your behaviors and attitudes.

Always remember to speak the truth out of an ocean of love, to best facilitate open and honest dialogue. Be mindful that "it's always too soon to quit," and that even the smallest positive changes that you make, can produce great hope and change of perceptions on the part of your partner. These changed perceptions create a new reality and refreshed responsiveness.

WOMEN. . .ASK YOURSELF. . .

DO YOU. . .	THEN SEEK TO. . .

KNEELING LEVEL

1. Realize that, no matter how you have been treated by your husband, and no matter how wrong he has been on many things, that it is possible that you have made mistakes as well? Because most women are "integrative" thinkers, who live in the past, present, and future all at the same time, you probably have great relational recall, which means you are often "right" about how things took place. But that doesn't mean you are always right. This great ability can be a curse if it instigates a superiority of innocence, and believing you're the only victim in this relationship.

1. Remember that a man needs to be admired and respected. He needs to feel like a "man." When a marriage is unhealthy, both parties feel like victims, even if it is more one than the other, who really is. Because men are compartmentalizing thinkers who "isolate," living in the present, while incidentally resourcing the past and future, he tends to think in the "let's start over" mode, often ignoring the pain of the past, almost as if it never occurred. This will greatly frustrate you and even anger you, because of the pain of remembrances. You will be greatly tempted continually to "unscramble the scrambled" yesterdays by reminding him of your pain, or the fact that he created it. In order to keep him from "giving up," because of your constant reminders of this being his fault, it is imperative that you focus on doing the "right thing" as opposed to "being right."

Your pride has been greatly wounded. It will continue to raise its growling head, as long as you let it, or even feed it. Pride is a sin that will keep you so focused on your right to be happy (which he has prevented), that it will push you towards being more selfish and more vengeful. In order to "do the right thing," you must do "right things." You do that by risking again and realizing all over again, that this relationship is not about you, but you and him. Who is at fault is no longer an issue. The issue now demands that self-focused pride be put away and other-focused willing vulnerability dominate our thinking as much as possible.

(HUMILITY)

WOMEN. . .ASK YOURSELF. . .

DO YOU. . .	THEN SEEK TO. . .

KNEELING LEVEL

2. Recognize that your attitude has greatly shaped your actions in the past, and that by having a new and different attitude, it can shape your actions in the future? Most women are much more in touch with their emotions than most men. Because women tend to be more emotional, they think and dwell on their feelings much of the time. Having had so many bad feelings about your marriage for so long, makes it difficult to be thankful, especially when you feel just the opposite. Watch out for "stinkin' thinkin'." The wounds you have are deep. That makes you dangerous when it comes to how you feel he should be treated. At times you're going to want to let him know how he made you feel, because you want him to feel the same things. That is revenge, not humility. It is pride

2. Turn "sorrow into a song." There are "no accidents," only incidents that can influence and control the purposes of your life. God is not surprised by any of the occurrences of your life. Certainly, He did not cause the bad ones, but He has allowed them in His permissive will. His plan for you is to utilize everything (even the bad), in bringing you closer to Him, His will, and a greater plan for your life than you have previously experienced. Think thanks! Make a list of 7-10 items you like about your husband (even if it's small things) and thank God for each item on this list at least three times a day. Determine to not criticize or complain. Try not to be negative or elevate your voice to a different range or tone (mother voice). Notice positive things and compliment him on them. This approach will help you appreciate him

and produces nothing but more pain. You cannot move forward if you choose to continually go back.

all the more and serve to additionally motivate you. The more you use this approach, the quicker your heart will begin to soften, which is absolutely essential.

(THANKFULNESS)

WOMEN. . .ASK YOURSELF. . .

KNEELING LEVEL

DO YOU. . .	THEN SEEK TO. . .
3. Feel like a hypocrite for trying to have a thankful attitude, when your spirit is muttering under its breath, "Thankful? Like heck I am!" It is natural and normal, just not productive. When you've emotionally "risked it all" and feel as though your very soul has been trashed, violated, and stepped on, it is natural to believe that "it's all about you." Your world was ripped out from under you (and maybe the world of your children) and it sure feels like somebody has to pay, and it isn't going to be you (or the children) anymore. Your world has become very introspective and it is difficult to see a bigger and brighter picture, but you must. You must see the value of a family that like the phoenix, has risen from the ashes; one that is stronger, more loving, and more influential, because of the battles fought and the lessons learned. You must look	3. Remember that forgiveness has been provided for you by a holy God. Being human, and therefore highly imperfect, you don't deserve it. None of us do. God's grace has been bestowed upon you as a model, and example, of what you must pass on to others. If you don't deserve it, but yet receive it, why not this man you hold so much against. By thinking big picture, and what could yet still be, you can have a thankful attitude that you both can have another chance (remembering you've both been hurt in some way). Forgive him. I know you've probably tried before and it hasn't worked well. You must forgive him continuously, not just as an event, but a process. Forgiveness fails without seeing the big picture of God's plan and what has been allowed, for a greater purpose. Therefore, coupled with thankfulness, forgiveness becomes a mighty force in defeating the bad and the ugly, and

to the value of what could be, instead of the fear of what once was. Remember you are not in this alone; he is willing and trying to be the man you once only dreamed about.

new good emerges from the ashes. It is a good that will, given the choice and the chance, can and will create surprising new beauty in your life.

(FORGIVENESS)

WOMEN. . .ASK YOURSELF. . .

DO YOU. . .	THEN SEEK TO. . .

FEELING LEVEL

4. Feel paralyzed by the thought of genuinely opening your heart and your spirit one more time? Do you still recall the moment or time that you actually emotionally "shut down" to any hope, any chance, any deep feeling for this man. Do you remember telling yourself that "I can't do this anymore" and finally meaning it. It was as if the pain of caring was so anguishing that you either had to stop caring or die. Somehow, within the deep recesses of your soul (and after possibly giving great thought or even attempted deed to marital death), your only good alternative was necessary, but exhaustive survival. You slammed the door of loving and allowed bitterness and indifference to rule the day and a shriveled up meaningless existence to rule the night. While you thought this was all behind you, this healing venture

4. Encourage him. He can't do it without your help. He's prone to give up if he sees negative reaction or little response. I know this feels hypocritical, because you don't feel like it, but it must be done. After all, there are some things in life that don't feel right, but are right. While you are deeply in touch with your feelings, they are not always accurate. Instead of being driven by your feelings at this time, exercise your faith, and utilize your will. An unknown author once penned these great words about "risking."

"To laugh is to risk appearing the fool. To weep is to risk appearing sentimental. To reach out for another is to risk involvement. To expose feelings is to risk exposing your true self. To place your ideas, your dreams, before the crowd is to risk their loss. To love is to risk not being loved in return. To live is to risk dying. To hope of restoring this bedeviled wasteland, has brought it all back. Yet it is no good. These thoughts only jeopardize this "beginning again." It only serves to self-indulge in victimized "pity parties," that are free, but very, very costly. He is really, really seeking to be different. You must give him a chance. If this really is authentic, if he really does want to love you the way you need to be loved, imagine what it might be like (with your help of course), if he makes it happen. After all, you've already invested a significant amount of time, emotion, and energy in him. Wouldn't it be better to reclaim the memories of the good times and recreate brand new great times, than start over with someone else, whom you know little or nothing about, or just go it alone in an uncaring, dangerous world?

is to risk despair. To try is to risk failure. But risks must be taken because the greatest hazard is life is to risk nothing. The person who risks nothing, does nothing, has nothing, and is nothing. He or she may avoid suffering and sorrow, but simply cannot learn, feel, change, grow, love, and live. Chained by his or her certitudes, he/she is a slave. He/she has forfeited freedom. ONLY A PERSON WHO RISKS IS FREE!" What fabulous truth. Every time we cross the street, get into our car, or fly in a plane, we risk our life's future. God wants to heal your marriage. Why not risk it all one more time? By risking it all, you will know beyond any shadow of doubt that you've tried it all before. Maybe you've tried, but probably not with him this committed to change. Carefully help him to prioritize and relate to you in a more tender, emotionally honest manner. Don't expect too much too soon. Events are easier. He's not as good at process as you are. Only a person who risks is free.

(RISK)

WOMEN. . .ASK YOURSELF. . .

DO YOU. . .	THEN SEEK TO. . .

FEELING LEVEL

5. Find yourself critical and fault-finding, regarding his attempts to show evidence of his love? Have you become more independent of him, because of your previous emotional release? Has this independence made you more controlling in terms of wanting things your own way? Do you desire now to be served rather than serve (after all, he has to prove himself worthy of your caring again)? Are you still finding ways to "keep him at arm's length?" Are you at all concerned about what others think of you? Have people you previously confided in seemed distant or unapproving? Does it bother you a lot? This is not abnormal. It is just your sinful pride worried about all the wrong things. Some people really care and don't want you to be hurt. Some just want to influence and control

5. Trust in the evidence of how he is attempting to treat you differently. He hasn't consistently traveled this road (if ever) in a long time. Trust in the fact that God is at work in changing his heart. A church that reaches out personally and sincerely could be of great help. Good Christian counseling is not always easy to find, but if you find it, seek to avail yourself of this wise counsel. No one endures without hope. Hope gives us the ability to dismiss deceitful fears and gives us confidence and faith to go on. Hope will energize your emerging belief in your husband and this marriage. Additional help and caring support systems, who are all working for the marriage should be pursued, as long as they don't alter your focus. Avoid the nay-sayers who pull you down and instill doubt. They will poison your thinking and sour your motivated enthusiasm. Warm up

you, believing that men are no good and you can't trust any of them. Some of them (who themselves have failed in relationship) relish your failure, so that their misery will have company.

to him, brag on him, positively reinforce every new and wonderful effort he makes. This will keep him motivated and help you to "believe." Remember, that men always feel good about your admiration and respect, even when they don't tell you.

(HOPE)

WOMEN. . .ASK YOURSELF. . .

DO YOU. . .	THEN SEEK TO. . .

FEELING LEVEL

6. Feel your heart stirring again? Have you begun to believe in him for the first time in a long time? Has he listened to you? Do you listen to him? Have you stopped responding in anger most of the time? Have you begun to see his virtues? Are you beginning to laugh at some of his comments? Do you sense that there just might be some fun in this marriage again? Are you sexually becoming interested or more responsive? Are you more and more looking for ways to please him?

6. Be patient. This can feel at times like a snowball rolling down hill. It may feel like your feelings and hopes are gaining momentum with surprising speed at times. Be patient. He's still a man who compartmentalizes and sometimes reverts to old habits or forgets your needs. You'll be immediately disappointed and feel as if you've been tricked. Be patient and softly and firmly discuss what happened, not trying to criticize but gently remind him of what went wrong. Discuss it and refresh his memory on what works and why. Be patient and help him habituate these new strategies. He will want to succeed. Be sure you indicate your admiration and respect for him often. Compliment him on his masculine strength, his appearance and manner of dress, his love for the Lord, his athletic ability and coordination, sense of humor, courage, tenderness and even his sexual capacities.

He needs to feel like a man. Encourage him in the things he enjoys doing. Take interest in as many of them as possible, without cultivating a breakdown in the new priorities that have been established. Ask him what he wants you to do to be a better partner. You are on your way.

(RESPONSE)

WOMEN. . .ASK YOURSELF. . .

DO YOU. . .	THEN SEEK TO. . .

HEALING LEVEL

7. Notice that you are more vulnerable now than you've been in a long time? Do you feel safer with him? Do you even want to sit close to him again? Does he sense your warming? Do you show it? Is there evidence of "dependent sweetness" in your tone of voice? Might he be wondering if somehow you have invented and consumed some sort of "happy pill?" Remember, it matters little if you feel these things, but don't show them. It's not unlike any complaints you've previously made when he told you he loved you, but didn't show it. Sometimes, it is difficult to believe that men have feelings too. Women often think that because they don't show it, they must not feel it. Most men are not as emotionally articulate enough to describe their frustrations and feeling misunderstood. They too can feel lost and unappreciated.

7. Be sure about his longings. Oh I know, you think you know what they are. There might be some obvious ones, but it is good to remember that they just might be different, now that the constant battles are over. Certainly, you might even be in a different season of your life, whether it be circumstance-related, or even age-related. Of course there are many books available to inform you of his needs, but you would benefit greatly just by asking him. This is a good time to find out what he longs for from you (pay close attention). Ask him how much he needs to feel that he's "in charge." Ask how you can make it happen and still maintain your own identity. Discuss it until it makes sense. Ask him how you can make him feel like a "winner" (that doesn't mean letting him win at games). Find out about his needs to be productive. Discuss how to differentiate between "nagging" him and "encouraging" him.

Sometimes a man can feel as if he is either "in trouble" or "about to be." You can change that.

Ask him how you can be more involved in his world, without suffocating him. Discuss how he can help you feel close to him, without him feeling smothered and gasping for a little space. Follow through. Write these things down to resource them. I know your relational memory is usually better, but this is crucial information. You can't afford to forget any of it. If you can do this in a "getaway" location, the easier it will be. This will feel like an ointment to your soul. There really could be a "soul mate" in him (even if he doesn't like the term). Let the real healing begin.

(TRUST)

WOMEN. . .ASK YOURSELF. . .

DO YOU. . .	THEN SEEK TO. . .

HEALING LEVEL

8. Sometimes find yourself compromising in your mind what you see evidence of, with your eyes. Compromise is the obstacle that eradicates closeness. You need to feel close to your man. You want so desperately to be able to truly believe in him. He has you almost there. You're having lengthy periods of serious trust that he is real and his love is real. However, because you never lose the ability to integrate past, present, and future (which is great in helping you be the emotional protector of the family), you still have flashback moments and things that remind you of some negative experiences from the past. There's the occasional "Don't get too hopeful girl, because this can change at any minute" kind of thoughts. The truth is, that if you are looking for him to always make you feel "first" in his life, he will fail you. As a compartmentalizer, driven by tasks,

8. Continually pray for him. Be righteous, but not self-righteous. Your focus should be on all the things that he is and has become, not on what he isn't. Praise him and appreciate him. When everything is measured by how it affects you, there's usually not much thought given to him. When you praise him, not only do it verbally with him, but also with others. Mental praise of him will instigate and rejuvenate your positive thoughts about him. Remember that your central nervous system is designed so that your attitudes and behaviors greatly influence your thinking. Do what you do well. Work on some things that you typically do not do well. Seek to please him. Put him in front of the rest of your family (children included). Just as he should put you first, so too should you do the same. It is a biblical principle and therefore never fails. Be efficient in meeting his needs. Learn more about him.

he is not designed to think of you constantly. Don't expect perfection, encourage performance. He can and will be great, but not always. I might add, that as wonderful as you are, you are probably not always amazing in how you respect and admire him. You must "cut him some slack." Your marriage is not intended to be a staid snapshot of personal perfection. It should instead be an unfinished mural of two lively souls, two lovers (and their children), with purpose and priority, traveling the pathway of life, on a journey that enjoys the mountaintops and endures the valleys, with rugged determination and hopeful anticipation.

Read books about men in general, and about their needs during different seasons of life. This will give you a more accurate picture of this man you chose to be the man of your life. Do this even if you don't see him doing the same thing. Many men hate reading. You might however get him to listen to a podcast. Surprise him from time to time. Everyone enjoys pleasant surprises, though they rarely ask for them. Don't spend time with negative women who have bad marriages. They'll pull you down and hold you back. You're stepping out and looking up! Keep on keeping on! Be proud of yourself. God is proud of you.

(FAITH)

WOMEN. . .ASK YOURSELF. . .

DO YOU. . .	THEN SEEK TO. . .

HEALING LEVEL

9. See his dedication for what it is? Have you noticed that more and more he indicates that he cherishes you? Oh maybe not the wild-eyed, heart-thumping manner he might have expressed when you first met, but a deep and authentic consideration of you and your feelings. You really, really matter to him. All the more, he wants to enter into your world and the "mystery" of who you are. There is much more flattery and praise than before. He actually takes serious time to listen to you. He may still give you advice (that you may or may not act upon), but he wants to help you. Do you occasionally initiate intimate moments spontaneously? Have you helped him understand that non-sexual touching is even more important (at times) than sexual touching? Do you give him positive eye contact, so that the two of you might begin to look into each other's soul again?

9. Submit to him. That means to serve him, no matter what, unless of course his expectation is blatantly sinful. A great synonym for submit today is abide. Abide in him, because by serving you, he is abiding in you. Naturally, the more you abide in each other, the more you please and abide in God. As you serve him and meet his needs, he becomes less vulnerable to external temptation and more spiritually and emotionally interconnected with you. Support him and create opportunity for fun together. Never let things get stale. Dream together. Set goals together. Work on projects together (if possible). Always vacation together! Be sure you have mutual bank accounts together (solidifies trust). Become his best friend and confidant. As you live for each other, you will be unstoppable, impregnable, and irresistible. People will beat a pathway to your door to find out the secret of your incredible marriage. Put on the

Are you reserving enough energy for him at the end of the day? Does he feel that no matter what, you believe in him?

cloak of humility, be thankful, be discerning, be forgiving, and be gracious. Your devotion and his dedication, with God's guidance and protection will serve to be a stunning model and revealing portrait of relational restoration and marital success. Congratulations!

(DEVOTION)

"I am my beloved's and my beloved is mine. . ."

Song of Solomon 6:3

CHAPTER FIVE

"DECISIONS"

*D*ecisions! Decisions! Decisions! Everyday in everyway, all we do is make decisions. Even when we become passive and refuse to make a decision, we're making a decision, a decision to do nothing.

Congratulations! "Marital Death" is dead!! By your decisions, you now have created an environment of trust and happy times. It is not perfect, nor will it ever be, on this side of heaven. You now have an atmosphere where fun and spontaneity can actually take place, because the constant tension expectancies, have given place to extreme communication, genuine warmth, self-vulnerability, and continual forgiveness. There's an appreciation and esteem for how far you've both come. You are more positively expressive in your thoughts and deeds. You are more cognizant of how generous your partner is, especially in the little things. You are so enjoying it when you know you've pleased your spouse. You are both actually able to discuss things without hysteria or yelling. You are maturing into what God always intended from the beginning. Disagreements (they'll still occur) are much more readily solved right away. Your ability to "forget about it" has increased dramatically, realizing that there are very few "hills you are willing to die on" anymore. You are experiencing "Marital Life" on an ongoing basis. You are making decisions all over the place. You are deciding how to act, think, believe, and even feel. Sometimes it is hard to believe that the two of you are the same people.

No matter how good or great it is, don't get careless. Keep setting goals together, plan for and work on projects together, dream together, play together, and enjoy your personal times and family times together. Be reflective together and keep learning from each other, about each other, and for each other.

Make conscious decisions to be loving, understanding, and accountable to each other. Communicate about time, money, people, plans, and feelings. Decide to always speak the truth caringly, from a heart of overflowing love. Decide to remember the former traps and triggers that sent your hopes spiraling downward, and be sensitive to communicate any negative potential to these happening again.

Yes, your decisions for the most part have been wise and great decisions. You can only maintain "Marital Life" by maintaining an attitude of humility. This is not something you can pray for, it is instead something you choose to be, humble.

Humility is energized and actualized by deciding to be meek. Meekness has been referred to as deciding to "give up your personal rights, to assume your personal responsibilities." Just think of it, if you decide to live for your partner, no matter what, and your partner decides to live for you, no matter what, you will both decide to "abide" in each other, by living for each other. This can be done, and it must be done.

As a realist, nobody does it 100% of the time, because of life's occasional turmoils, timetables, and tyrannies. But the secret of your "Marital Life" success is found in this mutual servanthood. The more you decide to do it, the easier it becomes. The more you both communicate your interest about serving each other, the less vulnerable your marriage will be to any adversity. The more you mutually decide to live for each other, the more people will marvel at the happy example you have set, and the more they will want to know your secret.

But how will you decide to respond? What will you say? To whom will you give the credit? Surely you didn't do it alone. Certainly God was and is a constant gardener of your fruitful "Marital Life." There are always two parts to everything, your part and God's part. You had to be willing; He had to be wanting. You had to be deciding; He had to be delivering. You had to be persistent; He had to be protective. You had to be solving; He had to be saving.

You may ask, I get the solving part, what about the saving part? What do you mean? We know that God hates divorce (not people who divorce), because of the ruination of covenant, people and purposes. He loves us and wants to bless and save marriages, if at all possible. He loves you and wanted to help save your marriage, which He did. But even more than saving your marriage, God was interested in saving you, your spouse, and your family. Perhaps you are all already "saved." If so, you know what I mean. If you're not sure, the following will help you understand.

It's really all about the decision that God made. . .somewhere in eternity past. Because of God's decision, it enables us to make our decision. For us, it all began when sin came into the world.

Because sin came into the world, mankind could no longer have a relationship with God. **God had a problem that only He could solve**. How could a **perfect God** allow **imperfect people** (Romans 3:23) into a **perfect Heaven** for a **perfect eternity?**

Since **God is holy and perfect**, He can only accept a **perfect offering**. We are **imperfect** and unable to provide that, but God loved us so much, that He did it for us. God sent part of Himself, His Son, Jesus Christ, to shed **His perfect blood** on the cross of Calvary. We know this to be true because the Bible says in **John 3:16 "For God so loved the world that He gave His only begotten Son, that whosoever believeth in Him should not perish, but have everlasting life."**

Listen! It is imperative that we fully grasp that the term **"believeth in Him"** implies far more than the "intellectual approval" given today, to anything we acknowledge to be true.

Today the word **"believe"** has evolved into a term meaning general agreement, but the **original meaning** of the word means we are to totally **accept, receive, and entrust ourselves** to what we believe. **IT IS AN UNCHANGEABLE DECISION!**

When we actually pray to invite Christ into our life, the Bible **guarantees** that He becomes closer than a brother because He actually comes to live inside us. In **Revelation 3:20**, Jesus says, **"Behold I stand at the door and knock, if any man hear my voice, and open the door, I will come into him and be with him and he with me."**

After making this **faith decision** and praying to **receive** Christ into our life, the Bible assures us that we **have** forgiveness of all sin and a guaranteed home in Heaven. **WHAT WILL YOUR DECISION BE?**

It doesn't take a **perfect person** to get into Heaven, but it does take a person who comes to know a **perfect God.** Jesus said in **John 14:6, "I am the way, the truth, and the life, no one comes unto the Father, but by me."** We can only be acceptable to God by inviting Christ to come into our life, asking Him to forgive us of our sins, and pledging, with His help, to live for Him. When we make this decision, He **will** come in and **never** leave us or forsake us (Hebrews 13:5).

Friend, it is not mysterious, it is not magical, but **it is miraculous.** If you seriously and sincerely ask Jesus Christ to come into your life, the bible says He will come in (John 1:12). **MAKE THE DECISION NOW!**

Right now, if you want to be sure that you are a Christian (follower of Christ), and be certain that if you were to leave this world this very moment, that you would be absent from the body and present with the Lord (2 Corinthians 5:8), repeat this **decision** (really meaning it) to yourself:

A PRAYER OF DECISION
GOES SOMETHING LIKE THIS:

"Lord Jesus, I love You and I believe in You. Lord, I ask You to come into my life today and live in it. Give me triumph over my disbeliefs and my failures and forgive me for all of my sins. And when I leave this world, grant me a home in Your Heaven. Thank You, Lord

Jesus. Help me to live for You from now on. I ask it in Jesus' precious name."

"And now, Oh God, I pray that You will seal this prayer in my heart. Lord, I pray that what has taken place within me shall also take place outside of me, as I give up my sins and live my life; brand new; born again; saved; and knowing (1 John 5:13) that I am on my way to Heaven once I leave this world. Thank you for giving me Your Son. Bless me now and bless my family, for I ask it in Jesus' name. Amen."

For the Bible says "He that has the Son has life and he that has not the Son of God has not life (1 John 5:12)."

WHAT ASSURANCE!
WHAT HOPE! WHAT JOY!

Friend, of all the **DECISIONS** in life, this is the **ONLY ONE** that can change your **ETERNITY** and give you power for every day of your life.

How do I know? Because it has changed mine, and it can change yours.

Indeed, it is my fervent prayer that through the Marital Death/Marital Life process, you have made a decision personally and privately to entrust your life to the Lord Jesus Christ. If you already knew Him, because of that personal decision, then keep growing in your faith, your walk, and your service toward Him. He will certainly continue to successfully direct your paths as you "go and tell."

If you have made the decision to know Him and invite Him into your life today, I rejoice with you and enthusiastically welcome you into the family of God. Find an evangelical church, where this message of salvation through Christ alone is preached; get a Bible and begin reading from the Gospel of John in the New Testament portion; pray to our Lord often, speaking to Him in everyday language. He will hear, understand, and guide you. Trust Him, because He has an even greater plan for your life now. He loves you and wants to guide you, protect you, and bless you.

If you are one who has applied the processes, but choose to ignore or not believe in Jesus Christ for your salvation, I ask you to just remain open-minded about Him. If you are not yet convinced, He will reveal Himself to you in other ways. You are always on His mind and in His plans. I pray that you will one day meet Him on your journey, because He has brought you this far, for more than just a time as this.

A final word to all who have read this book. Remember that the process works when two people are willing. Be mindful that "it's always too soon to quit." "Work will have to be done, and only by strong fighting can your marriage (city) be redeemed."

DOSSIER
Of
Richard Robert George, BS, MS, MS

*R*ichard Robert George is from Buffalo, New York. He is presently the Shepherding Pastor at The Chapel at CrossPoint. His professional studies include a BS and MS degrees in Education from the State University College at Buffalo, and an MS Degree in Counseling from Niagara University. Rev. George has done additional study at Liberty University and The Christian Counseling and Educational

Foundation (CCEF) in Laverock, PA. He has a vast and varied background in Counseling, Education and Church Ministry, having worked extensively with married couples, youth and adults speaking at Conferences, Seminars, and Churches.

Richard has also authored and had published three books for children: *"Charlie and the Chocolate Factory: A Play"* . . . *"Charlie and the Great Glass Elevator: A Play"* . . . *and "James and the Giant Peach: A Play."* Additionally, he is a free-lance poet and author, having been published in the American Association of Christian Counseling Magazine, <u>Christian Counseling Connection</u>.

CPSIA information can be obtained at www.ICGtesting.com
Printed in the USA
BVOW071751061212

307472BV00001B/5/P